ICONS

KENDRICK LAMAR

REVOLUTIONARY IN RHYMES

CARLA MOONEY

TWENTY-FIRST CENTURY BOOKS / MINNEAPOLIS

Twenty-First Century Books™
An imprint of Lerner Publishing Group, Inc.
241 First Avenue North
Minneapolis, MN 55401 USA

For reading levels and more information, look up this title at www.lernerbooks.com.

Main body text set in Gill Sans MT Std.
Typeface provided by Monotype Typography.

Library of Congress Cataloging-in-Publication Data

Names: Mooney, Carla, 1970–author.
Title: Kendrick Lamar : revolutionary in rhymes / Carla Mooney.
Description: Minneapolis : Twenty-First Century Books, 2026. | Series: Icons | Includes bibliographical references and index. | Audience: Ages 13–18 | Audience: Grades 7–9 | Summary: "One of the most influential rappers of his time, Kendrick Lamar has greatly impacted hip-hop and musical storytelling. From his first mixtape to a Pulitzer award-winning album to activism and philanthropy, learn more about Lamar's career"—Provided by publisher.
Identifiers: LCCN 2025013645 (print) | LCCN 2025013646 (ebook) | ISBN 9798765688632 (library binding) | ISBN 9798348029616 (paperback) | ISBN 9798348000226 (epub)
Subjects: LCSH: Lamar, Kendrick, 1987-—Juvenile literature. | Rap musicians—United States—Biography—Juvenile literature.
Classification: LCC ML3930.L136 M66 2026 (print) | LCC ML3930.L136 (ebook) | DDC 782.421649092 [B]—dc23/eng/20241023

LC record available at https://lccn.loc.gov/2025013645
LC ebook record available at https://lccn.loc.gov/2025013646

Manufactured in the United States of America
1 – CG – 12/15/25

CONTENTS

INTRODUCTION
Winning the Pulitzer Prize 5

CHAPTER 1
Early Life and Childhood 8

CHAPTER 2
Early Career 16

CHAPTER 3
First Album 25

CHAPTER 4
Mainstream Success 31

CHAPTER 5
Artistic Growth 38

CHAPTER 6
Introspection and Artistry 46

CHAPTER 7
Soundtrack Success and a Break 53

CHAPTER 8
New Music, New Steps 61

CONCLUSION
Legacy and Impact 68

Glossary 70
Source Notes 72
Selected Bibliography 75
Further Information 76
Index 78

Introduction

Winning the Pulitzer Prize

In January 2018 hip-hop artist Kendrick Lamar came up short at the Grammy Awards. His groundbreaking fourth album, *DAMN.*, was nominated for the prestigious Album of the Year award. It was Lamar's third nomination for Album of the Year. Neither of the first two had won the award. Although *DAMN.* won five other Grammys, Lamar again didn't win Album of the Year. But a few months later, *DAMN.* won an even bigger award.

In April 2018 *DAMN.* won the Pulitzer Prize for Music. The moment made history. The Pulitzer Prizes are a group of annual prizes awarded for outstanding achievement in journalism, books, drama, and music. The music prize was first awarded in 1943. Until 2018 only classical or jazz artists had won the prize. Lamar became the first hip-hop artist to win.

DAMN. was a success with both fans and critics following

In addition to the Pulitzer Prize, Kendrick Lamar also won the 2018 Grammy Award for Best Rap Album for *DAMN.*

its 2017 release. It debuted at number one on the *Billboard* 200 chart and was one of 2017's most streamed albums worldwide. The album tackled issues of race, faith, identity, and the economic struggles of Black Americans. It blended Lamar's signature storytelling and poetic style with hard-hitting beats. The Pulitzer Prize music jury unanimously selected *DAMN.* as the winner. The album was more than music. It was a masterpiece.

Winning a Pulitzer for his music was an incredible moment for Lamar. The honor cemented his legacy as one of the greatest rappers and hip-hop artists of all time. Lamar also recognized that the award was more than an individual achievement; it was a recognition of the entire hip-hop music genre. "It's one of those things that should have happened with hip-hop a long time ago. It took a long time for people to embrace us—people outside of our community, our culture—to see this not just as vocal lyrics, but to see that this is really pain, this is really hurt, this is really true stories of our lives on wax. And now, for it to get the recognition that it deserves as a true art form, that's not only great for myself, but it makes me feel good about hip-hop in general," he said.

> **"It took a long time for people to embrace us."**
>
> *—Kendrick Lamar*

Lamar poses before the 2025 Super Bowl halftime show. *DAMN.* was a major step toward Lamar headlining the Super Bowl. His performance also marked the show's first solo rap headliner.

1

Early Life and Childhood

Kendrick Lamar Duckworth was born on June 17, 1987, in Compton, California. His parents, Paula Oliver and Kenny Duckworth, named their son after Eddie Kendricks, a cofounder of the musical group The Temptations. Oliver and Duckworth were originally from Chicago but had moved to Compton to escape violence in their neighborhood and build a better life. Money was tight for the young couple, but eventually they saved enough to rent a small apartment. After welcoming Kendrick, they later had two more sons and a daughter.

Oliver worked as a hairdresser, while Duckworth took various jobs. At times the family struggled to make ends meet and relied on government assistance such as food stamps (now called Supplemental Nutrition Assistance Program, or SNAP benefits). They also lived in Section 8 housing. Section 8 is a federal program that helps low-income families find safe

Lamar grew up in Compton. His experiences there provided inspiration for many of his lyrics.

housing. Oliver was honest with Kendrick about their financial situation. She used to walk him home from elementary school and answer his questions about government assistance programs and housing.

Childhood in Compton

Although Kendrick's parents hoped to leave violence behind in Chicago, Compton had its own problems. In the 1990s, Compton struggled with poverty, crime, and violence. Growing up in Compton, Kendrick saw many things that

Compton mayor Aja Brown (*left*) would award Lamar (*center*) the keys to the city in a ceremony honoring the rapper in 2016.

would later shape his lyrics and music. In his neighborhood, he saw violence, police brutality, and the effects of drug use on communities, especially the Black community.

When Kendrick was five years old, he witnessed the murder of a drug dealer outside his apartment building. It had a lasting impact on him. "Admittedly, it done something to me right then and there. It let me know that this is not only something that I'm looking at, but it's something that maybe I have to get used to," he said. A few years later, eight-year-old Kendrick was walking home from elementary school when he saw another man get fatally shot in the drive-through of a local fast food restaurant.

But Kendrick had a strong support system, and growing up in Compton brought good moments too. Kendrick credits his parents with helping him stay out of trouble and focus on school and music instead of violence and crime. Oliver often reminded her son not to let anything get in the way of his dreams. Duckworth took Kendrick to the local swap meet every weekend and talked to Kendrick about the mistakes Duckworth made growing up. Father and son also bonded over their mutual appreciation of rapper Tupac Shakur and rap music. Kendrick considered himself lucky to have his father present in his life when so many of his friends did not. Duckworth also taught Kendrick how to deal with his emotions instead of acting out.

Growing Up with Music

Music surrounded Kendrick from an early age. His parents played music from a wide range of artists at home. Their music provided the soundtrack to Kendrick's childhood and influenced his future musical career. They played artists

Tupac Shakur

Kendrick Lamar has pointed to legendary rapper Tupac Shakur as one of his influences. Born in 1971, Tupac was an iconic American rapper, actor, and activist known for his raw, poetic lyrics that addressed social issues, poverty, and injustice. Rising to fame in the early 1990s, he became a central figure in hip-hop with albums such as *Me Against the World* and *All Eyez on Me*. His outspoken nature and conflicts within the industry fueled the East Coast versus West Coast rivalry. The rivalry was between both artists and fans of the East Coast and West Coast hip-hop scenes, which cultivated and produced distinct styles of hip-hop music. The rivalry was at its peak in the mid-1990s. On September 7, 1996, Tupac was fatally shot in Las Vegas, Nevada.

Legendary rapper Tupac Shakur inspired Lamar to pursue a career in hip-hop music.

such as Big Daddy Kane, Eazy-E, Marvin Gaye, and the Isley Brothers. The different sounds broadened Kendrick's appreciation for various music styles.

In 1995 Kendrick went with his father to the Compton Swap Meet. Young Kendrick watched rappers Tupac Shakur and Dr. Dre film a music video for "California Love," a single on Tupac's 1996 album, *All Eyez on Me*. Eight-year-old Kendrick was in awe seeing the superstar rappers in person. The experience had a lasting impact on him and planted the seeds for Kendrick's future career in music. He was going to be a rap star.

Introduction to Writing

Kendrick was a quiet child who got good grades in school. He met English teacher Regis Inge in seventh grade. Inge introduced him to creative writing and poetry. Tensions were high in the Vanguard Learning Center school, as gang violence on Compton's streets often spilled into the school's hallways. Inge believed poetry could help his students express their emotions without turning to violence. Kendrick poured himself into creative writing and found an outlet for his emotions. "You could put all your feelings down on a sheet of paper, and they'd make sense to you. I liked that," he later explained.

Inge made Kendrick work hard on his writing. When Kendrick turned in his assignments, Inge often returned them with edits and pushed Kendrick to work even harder. Inge's critiques motivated Kendrick. He wanted to be the best and poured everything he had into his writing. Kendrick journaled his thoughts and wrote poems. He scribbled rap lyrics on notebook paper when he was supposed to be

Gang Violence in Compton

Compton struggled with gang violence when young Kendrick Lamar lived there. In the late 1960s the infamous street gang, the Crips, formed in south central Los Angeles. Before long a rival gang, the Bloods, formed in Compton. The two gangs clashed over territory over the years as growing unemployment and poverty triggered a rise in crime and street gangs. In 1988 the Compton rap group N.W.A. released their album *Straight Outta Compton*, which focused on gang life and police violence in Compton.

The Compton rap group N.W.A. poses for a picture with rappers The D.O.C. and Laylaw during the *Straight Outta Compton* Tour in 1989.

finishing homework for other classes. He wrote about the world around him, including drug use, gang violence, and life in Compton.

By the time Kendrick was in high school, his childhood goal was cemented: he would become a rapper. He practiced coming up with rhymes spontaneously. But when Kendrick was around sixteen, he began hanging out with teens who partied and drank alcohol. Several of his friends joined a gang. Kendrick did not, but he still got in trouble and had a few experiences with the police. The crowd he hung out with often broke into and robbed homes. His parents kicked him out of the house for two days after police told them he had taken part in a local robbery. All these experiences would serve as inspiration for his music.

2

Early Career

Before the world knew his name, Kendrick made music under the stage name K.Dot. K.Dot was an alter ego, a character that teenage Kendrick could embrace. He posted videos on YouTube spitting out rhymes and imitating the high-profile rappers at the top of the hip-hop industry, such as 50 Cent, OutKast, and Jay-Z. These early rhymes highlighted Kendrick's technical ability and natural cadence but lacked the lyrical authenticity of his later work.

First Mixtapes

At Centennial High School, Kendrick met Dave Free, another teen with an interest in the music industry. Dave had a makeshift recording studio in his garage, and he invited Kendrick to come over and try it out. "Everyone back then was talking about drugs," Free said in a 2012 documentary. "But he had this one line—'I ship keys like a piano,' or something like that, and I just thought that was the most amazing line for somebody his age." Dave decided that day he

Lamar attended the *Straight Outta Compton* movie premiere in 2015. He credits his experience growing up in the neighborhood as an inspiration for many of his lyrics too.

wanted to work with Kendrick.

Kendrick and Dave quickly bonded over their love of rap music and the television sitcom *Martin*. The two teens recorded music at Dave's garage studio and Dave's older brother's apartment. Kendrick began performing around this time too, putting on shows around the neighborhood, at a local comedy club, and even behind a tattoo parlor.

In 2003 Kendrick released his first mixtape with Dave credited as his DJ. Although the mixtape was not a

Lamar and his long-time friend and collaborator Dave Free would win the Best Music Video award for "Not Like Us" at the 2025 Grammy Awards.

widespread success, it highlighted Kendrick's raw talent and potential. Local rap enthusiasts began to take notice of the talented teen.

Top Dawg Entertainment

After high school Free worked as a computer technician, while still helping Kendrick with his music. One day Free got a call from Anthony "Top Dawg" Tiffith, the founder of Top Dawg Entertainment (TDE), a new independent record label. Tiffith needed a computer repair. Free admired Tiffith's attitude and determination to make his music label a success and knew it was a golden opportunity to get Kendrick's music in front of him.

When Free arrived at Tiffith's house, he realized within a few minutes that he was not going to be able to fix the computer. He slowly began taking the computer apart. While he pretended to work on it, Free played Kendrick's latest mixtape. He made sure it was loud enough for Tiffith to hear. By the time Free admitted he could not repair the computer, Tiffith was hooked. He wanted to hear more.

Lamar (*right*) enjoys a Los Angeles Clippers game with Tiffith in 2015. The two had become colleagues and friends.

Tiffith invited Kendrick to a live audition at his studio. It was the opportunity that Kendrick had been waiting for. Kendrick freestyled for nearly two hours at the studio. Tiffith immediately recognized Kendrick's potential. He quickly offered the young rapper a contract with TDE.

More Mixtapes and Local Buzz

In 2005 eighteen-year-old Lamar graduated from high school and signed a contract with TDE to work on an album. With TDE Lamar now had access to the label's recording studio in Carson City, California. Over the next few years, Lamar worked on refining his rap skills. He looked for inspiration from West Coast rappers, including Tupac Shakur and Ice Cube. In 2007 he released his second mixtape, *Training Day*, under his stage name, K.Dot. With TDE's assistance *Training Day* was better produced than Lamar's first mixtape.

Mixtapes

A mixtape is a collection of songs that an artist or listener puts together. In hip-hop an artist raps on a mixtape over beats that they or another hip-hop artist created. The first mixtapes were recorded on cassette tapes, which is where the name originated. Now mixtapes can exist in different media forms such as a digital playlist or a physical CD. Artists typically make a mixtape to give it away for free or sell it at a low cost to help them market their music and gain exposure in the music industry.

Lamar performs on stage at the 2015 BET Experience. Lamar's continued refinement of his early work and songwriting skills helped put him on stage with some of rap's top artists at the event, including Snoop Dogg and Jay Rock.

Lamar kept making music. Later in 2007 he released the mixtape *No Sleep Til NYC* with fellow TDE rapper Jay Rock. In 2009 he released his third solo mixtape, *C4*. He was still working under his stage name. Yet he increasingly felt it was time to introduce the world to Kendrick Lamar.

Introducing Kendrick Lamar

Later in 2009 Lamar decided to drop the name K.Dot. He explained, "It was a big epiphany. I woke up and called my dude Top Dawg—he owns Top Dawg Entertainment—and told him that I thought it was time for the people to know who I am. I've put out a lot of songs and mixtapes and they know that I can rap but they need to know my story. What is a man without a story?"

> **"I've put out a lot of songs and mixtapes and they know that I can rap but they need to know my story. What is a man without a story?"**
>
> *—Kendrick Lamar*

Lamar released his self-titled fourth solo mixtape, *Kendrick Lamar EP*, on New Year's Eve in 2009. Instead of trying to be the next Jay-Z or pretending to be his K.Dot alter ego, Lamar focused on his songwriting for the release. As Lamar's music became more popular, the underground buzz around the young rapper increased along with expectations for his next release. Lamar released another solo mixtape, *Overly Dedicated*, in 2010.

A Call from Dr. Dre

In 2010 Lamar traveled with the Independent Grind Tour as a hype man for Jay Rock. During a stop in Los Angeles, Lamar was eating at a restaurant with a friend when his phone rang with a number he did not recognize. It was a call from legendary producer Dr. Dre, who said he liked Lamar's music. At first Lamar thought the phone call was a prank. He promptly hung up. But then his phone started ringing off the hook with call after call from people linked to Dr. Dre. Lamar

Freestyle Rap

On many of his early mixtapes, Lamar used a style of rap called freestyle. Freestyle rap is a form of improvisational rapping where lyrics are created entirely or mostly spontaneously. Freestyle rap highlights a rapper's creativity, flow, and lyrical skill, often over a beat or acapella. Freestyle can involve wordplay, storytelling, or punchlines, sometimes incorporating elements from the surrounding environment or audience suggestions. It is a fundamental aspect of hip-hop culture, often seen in rap battles where MCs compete with clever rhymes and wit.

Lamar performs freestyle rap on stage at the 2012 Coachella Valley Music & Arts Festival in Indio, California.

realized that it was not a prank, and he had just hung up on an opportunity to work with one of his rap idols.

The call from Dr. Dre was life-changing. The next week Lamar was in the studio with him, working on vocals for one of Dre's upcoming projects. Dre gave young Lamar advice on topics from pronunciation to production. He also worked out a deal with TDE to bring Lamar into Dre's record label, Aftermath Entertainment.

Lamar joins Dr. Dre at the iconic rapper's Rock and Roll Hall of Fame induction ceremony in 2016.

3

First Album

After the Independent Grind Tour ended, Lamar retreated to concentrate on writing new music. After the chaos of tour life, he wanted to be somewhere he felt comfortable. He returned to Compton where his music had started.

Personal Inspiration

In the spring of 2011, Lamar wrote the songs for his first official album, *Section.80.* As he had done for his last two mixtapes, *The Kendrick Lamar EP* and *Overly Dedicated*, Lamar wrote lyrics that were personal to himself and the people around him. This time Lamar widened his lens to the struggle of his generation. He wrote about kids like him born in the 1980s who grew up with drugs, especially crack cocaine, impacting the neighborhoods where they lived and worked. He dove into their experiences, feelings, and struggles.

As he wrote, Lamar used his personal experiences as a young Black man in Compton for inspiration, along with those of his uncles and cousins. Lamar also tapped into the

Lamar poses with Jon Cohen and Andy Cohn of Fader Records at the FADER FORT by FIAT NYC music festival in 2011. Lamar performed songs from *Section.80* at the festival.

experience of a close friend who was sentenced to twenty-five years to life in prison for a violent crime. "He had no guidance and was caught in that negative stigma of our generation that [we] don't care about anything and don't listen to anybody," Lamar said. "He was so young and his life is almost completely gone . . . Just the fact that's gone from him at such a tender age shows me that we have a lot to go as far as listening and being able to critique ourselves as individuals." Lamar sought not only to represent this experience, but also to explore his grief in thinking he'd never see one of his friends again.

Recording *Section.80*

After a few months of writing, Lamar stepped into the studio to record his album. He later explained how he approached the recording process. "I don't really like to force things. If it don't come then and there I'll leave it alone and hopefully it comes back [whether it's] two hours later or a day later."

Lamar also talked about what the content of his albums represents. "The story of Kendrick Lamar is the story of a good kid in a mad city. It's about a boy trying to figure out the world. My records don't come off preachy, they come off as [me] trying to find answers. Maybe me and the listener can give each other answers and try to figure it out together," he said.

Lamar worked on *Section.80* under TDE. The team had grown by this time, and Lamar worked with new producers who brought in fresh ideas and sound, from jazz loops to drums. The producers engaged in a friendly competition to record the most-discussed song on Lamar's record.

Lamar released *Section.80* on July 2, 2011. As he had

Use of Profanity

Lamar frequently uses profanity in his lyrics. All his language creates a realistic portrayal of systemic oppression, personal struggles, and day-to-day life, especially in urban areas. Rather than including profanity for shock value, Lamar weaves it into his storytelling to convey emotion and authenticity. His albums use explicit language to express frustration and give voice to marginalized communities. While some people criticize Lamar's use of profanity as vulgar and unnecessary, many others recognize it as a powerful tool in his music.

As Lamar continued writing new music, he got new recognition. In 2013 he performed on the Yahoo! On the Road music tour, a traveling music festival.

planned while writing, his finalized songs showcased his peers as real people with real concerns and problems who felt pain and hurt like everyone else. Across the album Lamar wove themes of personal struggles, social justice, and the challenges that young Black Americans face. "When I go to these neighborhoods in Compton, people tell me, 'You did something that not only represents you but it represents all of us. Thank you for making this music that represents me, that represents my struggle.' That feels good to me," Lamar said about people's reactions to the album.

Many songs had their own specific focus. In the song "A.D.H.D.," Lamar spoke to the connection his generation had with drugs. He wrote about the substance dependency that spread throughout the neighborhoods in which he lived. Beyond common addictive substances such as marijuana and alcohol, Lamar's peers also struggled with addictions to prescription pills, cough syrup, and even video games. The lyrics resonated with listeners who encountered similar struggles with substance use and self-medication.

In "Keisha's Song (Her Pain)" Lamar highlighted the experiences of women in marginalized communities. The song tells the story of a young sex worker who faced a lifetime of sexual abuse and encounters with corrupt cops and dangerous clients before being murdered. The song spotlighted the realities of exploitation and abuse that some women experience. It also highlighted Lamar's storytelling skill and his willingness to give a voice to those who were overlooked in society.

Lamar also critiqued the systemic oppression he witnessed firsthand in Compton. Songs such as "Ronald Reagan Era (His Evils)" spoke to the impact of the Reagan administration's policies in the 1980s on inner-city communities such as Compton. In particular, Lamar spoke to how the administration's war on drugs (a government effort to reduce illegal drug use) and mass incarceration policies impacted Lamar's childhood neighborhood and others like it.

One of the most significant tracks on *Section.80* was "HiiiPoWeR," a song that became an anthem for Lamar's growing fanbase. In an interview, Lamar described "HiiiPoWeR" as more than just a song—it was a movement that was quickly spreading. He explained that the three Is in the word *HiiiPoWeR* represented heart, honor, and respect.

The track's powerful message, along with Lamar's

passionate delivery, made it one of the most memorable tracks on *Section.80*. It established Lamar as an artist who was not afraid to speak his mind on social issues.

Critical Acclaim and Rising Popularity

Although *Section.80* was based on Lamar's Compton experiences, it resonated with people across the country. People from Philadelphia to Chicago and more could relate to the stories and themes on the album about life and struggles in America. Critics gave the album positive reviews. Tom Breihan from the digital music magazine *Pitchfork* rated the album an eight out of ten. He described Lamar as a young thinker trying to describe the world as he saw it.

Section.80 peaked at number 113 on the *Billboard* 200 chart. In 2017 the album was certified gold by the Recording Industry Association of America, which meant that it had sold more than five hundred thousand copies. The album is recognized as a classic that served as a bridge between Lamar's early independent music and the groundbreaking studio albums he later released.

4

Mainstream Success

In early 2012 Lamar was making a name as a rising star in the rap industry. Rap icon Drake invited him to join Drake's Club Paradise Tour as an opening act. On the tour Lamar traveled across the United States and London, performing in front of large crowds in big arenas. This time he was more than a hype man for another artist. Lamar performed as a solo act. The tour helped Lamar introduce new people to his music. His fanbase began to grow.

A Major Label

In March 2012 Lamar took the next step in his music career and signed a major record label deal. The agreement was a joint venture between major labels Interscope Records and Aftermath Entertainment and Lamar's independent label TDE. Under the deal, Interscope, Aftermath, and TDE would jointly release Lamar's next album, *good kid, m.A.A.d. city.*

Lamar later explained that one of the main reasons he

Lamar performs at the San Jose State Event Center in March 2012.

signed the deal was Interscope's reputation for quality work. Interscope worked with major artists such as Eminem and 50 Cent to put out quality albums. These albums remained relevant and popular over time, which Lamar appreciated.

good kid, m.A.A.d city

In July 2012 Lamar released "Swimming Pools (Drank)," the first single on his upcoming new album. At first look the song appeared to celebrate excessive drinking, and its pop-like beats became a popular anthem at open-air summer festivals. But a deeper look into Lamar's lyrics revealed his struggle with his family's history of alcoholism and the peer pressure that often comes with drinking. The record hit number seventeen on the *Billboard* Hot 100 chart, making it Lamar's first big mainstream hit. Anticipation grew for the release of his upcoming album.

On October 22, 2012, Lamar released his second studio album, *good kid, m.A.A.d city*. Dr. Dre, who still saw great potential in Lamar's talent, was an executive producer on the album. Lamar's new album was a concept album that provided an intimate look into more of his experiences growing up in Compton. It featured some of Lamar's popular songs, including "M.A.A.D. City" and "Sing About Me, I'm Dying of Thirst."

A hip-hop concept album typically tells a story by weaving plots, developing characters, and exploring themes across its tracks. The album's lyrics and production work together to create a listening journey that engages the audience. On *good kid, m.A.A.d city*, Lamar created a concept album that loosely followed his adolescence as he maneuvered the streets of Compton. The album highlighted themes of survival, repentance, and redemption. Musical tracks intertwined with skits and voice messages from friends and family to bring to life the challenges of peer pressure, gang violence, and the struggle to find one's identity. "The story is about one day in the life of me and my homeboys. I really didn't want to make it song-by-song. Each piece, I want to trigger certain points where you make a connection. . . . You have to listen to it more times to live with it and breathe with it," Lamar explained.

Lamar sits in the crowd at the 2013 BET Hip-Hop Awards at the Atlanta Civic Center in Atlanta, Georgia. He won the BET Album of the Year Award for *good kid, m.A.A.d city* at the event.

Critical and Commercial Success

Upon its release, *good kid, m.A.A.d city* was met with critical acclaim. Critics praised Lamar's lyrical ability and storytelling and the album's cohesive narrative. *Pitchfork* music critic Jayson Greene wrote about the album's authentic feel, "This autobiographical intensity is the album's calling card. Listening to it feels like walking directly into Lamar's childhood home and, for the next hour, growing up alongside him."

The album debuted at number two on the *Billboard* 200 chart and sold 242,000 copies in its first week. Since its release, the album has spent more than twelve consecutive years on the *Billboard* 200 chart, making it the first and only rap album to do so. The album was also certified triple platinum, meaning that it sold at least 3,000,000 copies. It was a mainstream success.

Grammy Nominations

The success of *good kid, m.A.A.d city* reached new heights when Lamar received seven Grammy nominations for it, including Best New Artist, Best Rap Album, and Best Rap Performance. Many people expected Lamar to win several awards. Yet at the fifty-sixth annual Grammy Awards show in January 2014, Lamar walked away empty-handed. Fans,

Lamar performs songs from *good kid, m.A.A.d city* on stage at the BBC Radio 1Xtra Live in London, England. The BBC also named the album one of the top albums of 2012.

DMX

One of Lamar's early influences was DMX (1970–2021), an American rapper, actor, and songwriter known for his raw, gritty delivery and emotionally charged lyrics. Rising to fame in the late 1990s, DMX became a dominant figure in hip-hop with albums including *It's Dark and Hell Is Hot* and *. . . And Then There Was X*. His music was well-known for his strong, energetic raps. DMX's distinct growling voice and powerful performances set him apart. His influence on rap culture has inspired many artists, including Lamar. Lamar credits DMX with inspiring him to write rap lyrics as a young teen.

American rapper DMX is one of Lamar's early musical influences.

Lamar performs at the 2014 Grammy Awards with Imagine Dragons at the Staples Center in Los Angeles.

critics, and even other artists were stunned. Duo Macklemore & Ryan Lewis beat out Lamar in three of the four categories they were both nominated in, including Best Rap Album. After the awards show, Macklemore both texted Lamar and publicly admitted that he believed Lamar deserved the Best Rap Album award.

Despite the losses, the Grammy nominations proved that Lamar had reached a new level of recognition in the music industry. He was no longer just an underground rap sensation; he had joined the stage with mainstream rap artists.

5

Artistic Growth

In 2014 Lamar toured the United States with Kanye West, and the experience opened his ears to new music. Lamar had grown up listening to West Coast hip-hop music, so he had limited exposure to rap icons and Black musicians from other regions. On the tour bus, Lamar listened to jazz musicians including Miles Davis and Donald Byrd and funk icons such as George Clinton and Sly Stone. Lamar noted the freedom and creativity each of these musicians incorporated into their music. They were the type of innovative musician he wanted to be.

Exploring Black Music

For his next album, Lamar wanted to mix funk, soul, bebop, and jazz musical styles with hip-hop. He wanted the album to be authentically Black, from the musical styles it incorporated to the topics it covered. A trip to South Africa and a visit to Robben Island, where South African activist and politician Nelson Mandela was imprisoned for eighteen years, sparked

Lamar performs in Los Angeles as part of Kanye West's Yeezus Tour.

inspiration for the new album.

To accomplish his vision, Lamar brought in new collaborators that included soul icons Ron Isley and Lalah Hathaway and funk legend George Clinton. He enlisted hip-hop greats Dr. Dre, Pharrell Williams, Pete Rock, and Snoop Dogg. Lamar also recruited a crew of musicians who could smoothly shift between musical genres. And he brought on Terrace Martin, a producer and musician with experience in jazz and funk genres.

For two years Lamar patiently worked on each line, beat, and note until they felt right to him. He was not focused on making an album full of radio tracks or club playlists. Instead he wanted to make an album that someone could listen to repeatedly and discover new meaning with each new play.

To Pimp a Butterfly

In March 2015 Lamar released his third studio album, *To Pimp a Butterfly*. He chose the album's title to reflect the challenges of his new celebrity and the music industry's grip on its artists. If *good kid, m.A.A.d city* was a personal coming-of-age story, *To Pimp a Butterfly* was a powerful social-political statement. The album blended soul, blues, jazz, funk, and spoken word elements to create a tribute to Black musical traditions while also speaking on current racial and social issues. In addition to the spoken word interludes, the album featured live instrumentals and poetic monologues that tied the album's tracks together into an overarching story.

The album not only celebrated Black culture but also voiced the frustrations and experiences of Black Americans. For example, the track "The Blacker the Berry" confronted themes of self-hatred and racial injustice. Lamar explained that he started writing the lyrics after the 2012 murder of Trayvon Martin. Martin was an unarmed Black teen who was shot and killed by a neighborhood watch volunteer. In part of the song, Lamar also expressed his own struggles of feeling marginalized in US society. He rapped, "I mean, it's evident that I'm irrelevant to society. That's what you're telling me, penitentiary would only hire me." Then in the last line of the song, Lamar sparked debate by rapping about Martin's murder. The lyrics wonder why the narrator weeps for Martin when gang violence might lead them to kill another Black person and calls themself a hypocrite. Some people praised

Lamar signs copies of *To Pimp a Butterfly* during the 2015 promotional tour of the album.

Lamar for taking a stand against gang violence, while others criticized him for emphasizing Black-on-Black violence more than the injustice of police brutality.

"Alright" Becomes an Anthem

One track on *To Pimp a Butterfly*, "Alright," became an unofficial anthem for the Black Lives Matter (BLM) movement. The BLM movement began as a hashtag after Martin's murder. Within two years it grew to become a political and protest movement calling for the fair treatment of Black people

Supporters of the Black Lives Matter movement call for fair treatment of Black people and protest the deaths of several Black individuals at the hands of police during a 2015 protest in Cleveland, Ohio.

by authorities in the United States and worldwide. BLM protested the deaths of Black people such as Eric Garner, Michael Brown, Meagan Hockaday, and others who were all killed by police.

During the summer of 2015, hundreds of Black activists gathered for a three-day conference at Cleveland State University in Cleveland. It was the first time many of them had met face-to-face to discuss plans for future protests and actions. During a break someone put on Lamar's new song, "Alright." The song and its message immediately resonated with the auditorium full of people.

Not long after, BLM protesters began shouting the chorus from "Alright" at BLM protests and events: "We gon' be alright." It became a rallying cry for the BLM movement.

Protesters across the United States chanted the song's lyrics during protests against police brutality.

At a protest march in Denver, Colorado, "Alright" was on a playlist of songs chosen to unify the people. Protesters danced and marched to the song's beat as it played. "Music uplifts our community, and so we were playing different songs that have been our 'struggle anthems' to equality so that black people can say their lives matter. And so Kendrick's song is something that is a rallying cry," explained Tay Andersen, one of the march organizers.

One of Lamar's most iconic moments as a performer occurred during the 2015 BET Awards when he powerfully performed "Alright." Lamar delivered the song on stage in front of a backdrop of a graffiti-covered police car and an enormous American flag. The performance solidified "Alright" as a power anthem for the BLM movement and cemented its status as a rallying cry for justice and hope.

Award-Winning Album

Critics hailed *To Pimp a Butterfly* as a masterpiece. Some called it an instant classic. Journalist Micah Singleton wrote, "*To Pimp a Butterfly* is perfect. There's no other adjective that can properly convey its greatness. *To Pimp a Butterfly* is an immaculate amalgamation [mix] of rap, jazz, funk, soul, and spoken word. It cannot be restricted by a single genre. It's the latest evolution of Black Music, and it's nothing short of genius." Singleton noted the power of Lamar's music beyond entertainment and wondered if Lamar could one day become the Black community's next strong public leader, following prior figureheads such as Martin Luther King, Jr. and Malcolm X.

"Bad Blood"

In 2015 Lamar notched his first number one song on the *Billboard* Hot 100, a collaboration with Taylor Swift. The rapper contributed a guest verse to the pop star's song "Bad Blood" on her album *1989*. Swift spoke publicly about their collaboration and praised Lamar's creativity. She said that watching Lamar create and record was an incredibly inspiring experience for her. When Swift rerecorded "Bad Blood" for the release of her album *1989 (Taylor's Version)*, Lamar went into the studio and rerecorded his part so she could include it on the new album too.

Lamar collaborated with Taylor Swift on the pop star's chart-topping hit "Bad Blood."

Lamar accepts the Grammy award for Best Rap Album for *To Pimp a Butterfly* from rapper Ice Cube.

At the 2016 Grammy Awards, Lamar was nominated for multiple awards. He won Best Rap Album for *To Pimp a Butterfly*. He also won Best Rap Song and Best Rap Performance for "Alright." The previous year he had also won two Grammys for "i," the first single released from *To Pimp a Butterfly*.

Professionally Lamar was on the rise. But he was making a name for himself on another stage as well. Lamar was slowly becoming a political figure. He had not intended to be one, but *To Pimp a Butterfly* and songs such as "Alright" and "The Blacker the Berry" put Lamar squarely in the middle of the country's political discourse. Even President Barack Obama was a fan of the young rapper and his music.

Introspection and Artistry

As Lamar's celebrity rose, he slowly stepped back from public life. In 2016 he did not grant as many interviews and steered away from social media. But now that so many fans knew him, Lamar could not go out at all without attracting attention. Because of that, he chose to primarily stay out of the public eye entirely except when he had a performance. For some fans, this increased the aura of mystery around the talented rapper and made them want more music.

Inspiration and Writing

Around this time Lamar was already working on material for his next album. Inspiration for new material came from many places. During a trip to New York, Lamar and some of his creative team spent an entire day listening to Frank Ocean's *Blonde* album, which had just been released on iTunes. The

Lamar (*crouching*) and Bono, lead singer of U2, perform their song "XXX" at the 2018 Grammy Awards. The song includes a sample from the U2 song "American Soul."

group experimented with similar sounds in a jam session, and the track "YAH" was formed.

Lamar had also been talking with legendary rocker Bono from U2 about collaborating. Bono sent Lamar several song ideas and vocal tracks. Lamar and his producers went through Bono's material and built a new track around it, "XXX."

Lamar recruited Kid Capri, an iconic DJ and rapper, to work with him on the new album too. Capri was known for his nineties hip-hop mixtapes. Capri contributed vocals and spoken introductions to five tracks on the album.

Lamar and his producers spent months revising and perfecting each track. Some tracks, such as “Pride,” evolved over a year. “Element” had about twenty-five different versions before it was finalized. Many tracks changed every day.

The new album featured a long list of contributors. In addition to Bono and Kid Capri, guest artists included Rihanna, James Blake, and bassist Thundercat. Coproducers on the album included Lamar’s regulars such as Sounwave and DJ Dahi and newcomers such as Greg Kurstin, who had produced “Hello” by Adele. Often the album’s contributors did not know how their work would be used until they heard the final track.

For two months before the album’s release, Lamar and his producers basically ate, slept, and worked around the clock in

Spirituality

Lamar opened up about his spiritual practices in a 2024 interview. He explained that he starts each day by talking with God, a conversation that can continue throughout the day. Most days he also heads out for an early morning run. For him, pushing through the physical pain during the morning run helps Lamar stay grounded and mentally strong. Running also helps him get closer to his spirituality and understand its role in his life more fully.

Lamar and Rihanna pose backstage at the 2018 Grammy Awards, where the pair won a Grammy award for Best Rap/Sung Performance for their song "Loyalty."

the studio. They tinkered with and tweaked the sound, beats, and speed of each track. Finally in April 2017 Lamar released his fourth studio album, *DAMN.*

DAMN.

DAMN. told a story across fourteen songs and featured themes of religion, anxiety, intimacy, and political weariness. The album opened with Lamar delivering a spoken-word

Lamar performs on stage at the 2018 Grammy Awards, which he also attended as an award nominee for *DAMN*.

introduction. At the album's end, Lamar returned full circle with the first sentence of the introduction. Interscope head John Janick was blown away the first time he listened to the complete album. "I had heard a handful of tracks early on—I heard 'HUMBLE,' 'DNA,' 'Love,' just those songs on their own. But then when they came in and played the album from beginning to end, hearing the whole body of work, the way the album ends . . . it was spectacular," he said.

Kung-Fu Kenny

Kung-Fu Kenny is one of Lamar's latest alter egos, introduced in his 2017 album *DAMN*. Lamar refers to himself as Kung-Fu Kenny several times on the album. The alias was inspired by actor Don Cheadle's character in the movie *Rush Hour 2*. In the movie, Kenny owned a Chinese restaurant and showed off his impressive martial arts skills. Lamar explained in interviews that his Kung-Fu Kenny alter ego represents his journey to becoming a master of his music and craft, much like a martial artist sharpening their skills.

Lamar introduced his Kung-Fu Kenny alter ego on his 2017 album, *DAMN*.

DAMN. debuted at number one on the *Billboard* 200 chart and quickly became one of the most acclaimed albums of the year. It was not only a commercial powerhouse but also a critical success, praised for its storytelling and emotional depth. The album produced several hit singles, including "HUMBLE." The song topped the *Billboard* Hot 100 and became Lamar's first solo number one hit. By July the album had reached double platinum status, selling more than two million copies.

At the sixtieth annual Grammy Awards in 2018, Lamar received seven nominations, including Album of the Year and Best Rap Album for *DAMN.* and Record of the Year for "HUMBLE." He won five Grammys, including Best Rap Album for *DAMN.* and Best Music Video and Best Rap Song for "HUMBLE." With *DAMN.*, Lamar cemented his legacy and influence in the hip-hop world.

The artistry on *DAMN.* brought an even greater honor for Lamar with his Pulitzer Prize win. It was a historic moment for Lamar's career and the artistry of hip-hop as a whole.

7

Soundtrack Success and a Break

In 2018 the Marvel superhero movie *Black Panther* opened in theaters worldwide. The movie celebrated Black excellence and told the story of King T'Challa, the Black Panther, as he attempts to save his people and country from enemies. The film was a commercial and critical success, earning a Best Picture nomination at the Academy Awards. And there had been no one better suited to create the movie's soundtrack than Lamar.

When director Ryan Coogler approached Lamar about the *Black Panther* soundtrack in 2017, the rapper was unsure. At first Lamar agreed to come up with a few songs. But when he started watching parts of the movie, he noted parallels to his own life and work. "[The film's themes] reminded me of why I made *To Pimp a Butterfly*. It was survivor's guilt. You want to be homegrown and help folks back home and give them game. You want to be there for them but if you're there,

Lamar's fame and demand would continue to grow as he tried new styles and completed more projects. In 2019 he headlined the Tycoon Music Festival in Atlanta, Georgia.

then you can't go out and explore," he explained. Lamar also felt that the Black representation in the production, including the film's Black director and mostly Black cast, was important. "It was something I dreamed of as a kid. A superhero who looked like us, talked like us and liked the same music," he said.

Once he decided to take on the project, Lamar and his producer Sounwave started work in August 2017 while touring for *DAMN*. In just two months while on the tour, they came up with creative ideas and a framework for the soundtrack. Once the tour ended, they reached out to several musicians, including African musicians such as Babes Wodumo, Sjava, and Saudi, and North American stars such as SZA and The Weeknd, adding their talents to the album. The result was a soundtrack that reflected the movie's themes and honored its African cultural roots as much as the cultures of the African diaspora.

Giving Back to Compton

Throughout his career, Lamar used his success to help uplift his Compton community. He has donated to local schools, supported music and sports programs, and provided funding for after-school initiatives. Lamar has also partnered with organizations including the Compton Unified School District to invest in education and resources for young people. In 2016 he received the Key to the City of Compton for his positive impact. Through his music and philanthropy, he continues to inspire and empower young people, proving that success can be used as a tool for meaningful change.

Lamar has performed at all kinds of music festivals. Here he raps at the Day N Vegas hip-hop music festival in Las Vegas in 2021.

Black Panther: The Album debuted at number one on the *Billboard* 200 chart in February 2018. By May the soundtrack was certified platinum, meaning it had sold more than one million copies. The soundtrack was a critical success and earned several award nominations, including an Academy Award nomination for Best Original Song for "All the Stars." The soundtrack was also nominated at the Grammys for several awards, including Song of the Year for "All the Stars" and Album of the Year. The song "King's Dead" won the Grammy for best rap performance.

Whitney Alford

Whitney Alford has been a significant figure in Lamar's life, offering support throughout his career. The couple met in high school in Compton and have maintained a private relationship since. Alford has inspired many of Lamar's lyrics. For example, songs such as "She Needs Me" and "Determined" from the *Kendrick Lamar EP* feature lyrics about a woman who is described as a powerful force in his life. In 2022 Alford appeared with Lamar and their two children on the cover of *Mr. Morale & the Big Steppers*. Despite Lamar's fame, Alford keeps a relatively low profile and typically stays out of the spotlight.

Lamar (*right*) and his fiancée Whitney Alford

Lamar performs in Inglewood, California, at the Pop Out—Ken & Friends, a 2024 concert sponsored by pgLang and creative studio Free Lunch. Money raised by the concert was donated to local charities in Los Angeles.

Taking a Break

After *DAMN.* in 2017 and *Black Panther: The Album* in 2018, Lamar took a hiatus from making his own music that would last until 2022. He explored other interests during that time, including acting. Later in 2018 Lamar made a guest appearance on a television show.

In 2020 Lamar expanded his presence into the business world. He announced a new company called pgLang, which he cofounded with longtime friend Dave Free. The company name is a shortened form of the term *program language* and is a service company for artists and creators that specializes in music and visual media production. Since its launch, pgLang has written and directed ads for Calvin Klein, produced several short films, directed music videos for Baby Keem and Lamar, collaborated with Converse and Louis Vuitton, and more. In 2023 pgLang would win six Cannes Lions Awards for the short film *We Cry Together.*

Lamar also spent time making music with fellow artists. He appeared as a guest artist on tracks by artists such as The Weeknd, Baby Keem, Jay Rock, Future, and others. In 2022 Lamar also joined legendary rappers Eminem, 50 Cent, Dr. Dre, Mary J. Blige, and Snoop Dogg on stage at the Super Bowl halftime show. He made a surprise appearance at the 2022 Coachella festival and performed two tracks with Baby Keem during Keem's set.

Left to right: **Hip-hop stars Lamar, Eminem, Dr. Dre, Mary J. Blige, and 50 Cent perform during the 2022 Super Bowl halftime show.**

During his break from music, Lamar also became a father. He has always been very private about his personal life and relationship with his longtime fiancée, Whitney Alford. In July 2019 the couple welcomed their first child, a daughter named Uzi. Their son, Enoch, would be born in 2022.

Leaving TDE

Although Lamar wasn't putting out music during his break, he was still thinking about his musical career. In August 2021 Lamar surprised fans and announced that he was working on his last album with his label TDE. "As I produce my final TDE album, I feel joy to have been a part of such a cultural imprint after 17 years. The Struggles. The Success. And most importantly, the Brotherhood," he wrote in a message on his website. Lamar signed the message as oklama, which many believe to be a new alias that is a play on his name. Others have suggested that *oklama* is a Choctaw word meaning "my people."

Lamar had worked with TDE for nearly two decades. In 2022 TDE president Terrence Louis "Punch" Henderson talked about Lamar's decision to leave the record label. He believed that Lamar had grown as an artist and was ready to strike out on his own in the industry. "I don't even know if I would describe it that way as ready to leave, as more so ready to build his own thing. That's a grown man right now. We watched him grow from a teenager up into an established grown man, a businessman, and one of the greatest artists of all time. . . . So it's time to move on and try new things and venture out," he explained.

8

New Music, New Steps

In April 2022 Lamar delighted fans with a surprise announcement. Through a document posted on his website, he revealed that his fifth studio album and final album with TDE, *Mr. Morale & the Big Steppers*, would be released on May 13, 2022. It had been five years since Lamar had released a full-length solo album. Fans could not wait.

Mr. Morale & the Big Steppers

Lamar and longtime producer Sounwave worked on material for the new album throughout Lamar's five-year hiatus. Although Lamar's previous albums were personal, telling the story of his life in Compton and generational experiences as a Black American, he tapped into even more intimate issues this time. The album opened with the lines "I been goin' through somethin' / 1855 days/ I been goin' through somethin.'" With this introduction Lamar set the stage for the album's core theme: despite his success, he still struggled with trauma. The album was structured as a therapy session, in which Lamar explored the causes and effects of his trauma, along with the trauma of his peers and community, and searched for a way to move forward.

In 2022 Lamar talked about carrying the beginnings of *Mr. Morale* inside himself for a long time. "It's stuff that I've written that's just now seeing daylight, because I wasn't secure with myself in order to do it. . . . It was really about not being insecure [or] tormented by opinions. When I did this, it was kind of the marker and the growth of everything I've always wanted to say. I think that was really my purpose of writing my way out of things that I was feeling, from the time I was 9 years old, all the way up to 35," he said.

Lamar admitted the album, which narrated his therapy journey through trauma, sex addiction, infidelity, accountability, and self-exploration, was not always easy for him to listen to because of its difficult topics. Songs such as "Mother I Sober" and "Father Time" explored generational cycles of abuse, while "Crown" explored Lamar's struggles with fame and the pressure it put on him.

To create the album, Lamar brought together a large group of producers, sound engineers, and instrumentalists, including longtime partners DJ Dahi, Beach Noise, Sounwave, and J.LBS. Many rappers create new material in a step-by-step process. First a producer sends a beat, and the rapper will write lyrics to it. Next they will record in the studio, and an engineer will add any finishing touches. For Lamar the process on *Mr. Morale*, like all his work, was more collaborative, bringing people together to create. Instead of working individually, Lamar's collaborators shared ideas, experimented with sounds, and made music until they hit upon the sound that felt right.

Critics praised *Mr. Morale & the Big Steppers* for its honesty, lyrical depth, and raw exploration of personal struggles, even when it ventured into uncomfortable areas. "*Mr. Morale & the Big Steppers* sees Lamar delivering performances teeming with intimacy and introspection: true emotion. Everything about the album feels authentic, every word, every thought process, and every melody culminating into an album that sacrifices 'perfection' in the name of truth," wrote arts and entertainment editor Lucien Clough. Lamar received eight Grammy nominations for *Mr. Morale & the Big Steppers*, including Album of the Year. He won three awards, including Best Rap Album, Best Rap Song for "The Heart Part 5," and Best Rap Performance for "The Heart Part 5."

Lamar accepts the Grammy award for Best Rap Album for *Mr. Morale & the Big Steppers*.

Feud with Drake

In the early years of Lamar's career, he collaborated with star rapper Drake on several projects. Lamar appeared on Drake's 2011 track "Buried Alive Interlude," while Drake appeared on Lamar's 2012 "Poetic Justice." Over the years the good feelings between the two artists slowly began to unravel. In 2013 Lamar called out several rappers, including Drake, on Big Sean's "Control" track when he rapped, "I got love for you all, but I'm trying to murder you. Trying to make sure your core fans never heard of you." Drake responded in an interview, denying that Lamar was out-succeeding him on any platform.

In the following years, Lamar and Drake traded jabs and disses with each other. Then in 2024 the feud exploded as the two artists engaged in a series of disses on various tracks. For example, in April 2024 Lamar released "euphoria," a more than six-minute track that disses Drake's rapping skills, his use

History of Diss Tracks

A diss track is a song that is intentionally disrespectful or mocking to others, usually other musicians. Diss tracks became popular in hip-hop in the 1980s. However, they also appear in other music genres. Artists such as Taylor Swift, Queen, and Lynyrd Skynyrd have all released diss tracks. For example, Lynyrd Skynyrd released the hit song and diss track "Sweet Home Alabama" in 1974 to call out fellow artist Neil Young for perceived insults in Young's earlier songs "Southern Man" and "Alabama."

of artificial intelligence, his racial identity, and his parenting skills. The title was a reference to an HBO television series for which Drake was an executive producer. In May Drake responded with a nearly eight-minute response that accused Lamar of infidelity and abuse in his relationship with his fiancée. Within a day Lamar responded with a track that took aim at Drake's parenting, accused him of having a secret daughter, and labeled him as a predator without explanation.

Then on May 4 Lamar dropped a new single, "Not Like Us." In the song he went further in his accusations against Drake. By May 18 "Not Like Us" hit number one on the *Billboard* Hot 100 chart. It spent fifty-three weeks on the chart and ended the year as 2024's number six song. It also topped streaming charts, landing at the top of Apple Music's 2024 global song chart.

GNX

Lamar took the music industry by surprise when he dropped a sixth studio album, *GNX*, in November 2024. The twelve-track album appeared on streaming services with little fanfare prior to its release. The album's name came from a 1987 Buick GNX, which appeared on the album's cover and was from the same year Lamar was born. *GNX* was Lamar's first album after leaving TDE. Instead *GNX* was released through pgLang. It was also released under an exclusive license with Interscope Records.

GNX was a tribute to Los Angeles and featured the city's distinctive G-funk sound across its tracks. A close group of collaborators worked with Lamar on the album, including Mustard, who also produced the wildly popular "Not Like Us," and Jack Antonoff, who had worked with numerous pop

2025 Super Bowl Halftime Show

Kendrick Lamar headlined the 2025 Super Bowl halftime show on February 9, marking the first time a rapper led the performance as a solo act. Celebrities including actor Samuel L. Jackson, singer-songwriter SZA, and tennis star Serena Williams joined him on stage for parts of the show. Lamar's setlist included the Grammy-winning "Not Like Us." His performance showcased his artistic prowess but also reignited discussions about the themes addressed in his songs. The Super Bowl appearance significantly boosted Lamar's music sales and streaming numbers, with multiple albums reentering the charts.

Lamar performs at the 2025 Super Bowl halftime show.

artists including Taylor Swift. On *GNX* Lamar was able to craft songs with mainstream appeal that also featured LA sounds.

GNX debuted at number one on the *Billboard* Hot 200 chart, making it Lamar's fifth number one album. It had the equivalent of 319,000 first-week unit sales in the United States, which included 380 million streams and made it one of the biggest debuts of 2024. Tracks from *GNX* shot up the *Billboard* Hot 100 chart and took over the chart's top five spots all at once with the songs "Squabble Up," "TV Off," "Luther," "Wacced Out Murals," and "Hey Now." Only three other artists had accomplished that feat: The Beatles, Taylor Swift, and Drake.

Grammy Triumph

Lamar's diss track "Not Like Us" was nominated for seven Grammy awards in five separate categories. At the February 2025 awards ceremony, Lamar dominated. He won in every category in which he was nominated, bringing home awards for Record of the Year, Song of the Year, Best Rap Performance, Best Rap Song, and Best Music Video.

Lamar accepted the prestigious Song of the Year award on stage from music legend Diana Ross. In his acceptance speech, Lamar credited West Coast rap pioneers and gave a shout-out to several former TDE label artists. He spoke about the power and culture of rap music. "This is what it's about man, because at the end of the day, nothing is more powerful than rap music. We are the culture, it's gonna always stay here and live forever," he said. Lamar also encouraged younger rappers to respect hip-hop's history and culture, saying, "I just hope you respect the artform, that's all. Respect the artform, it'll get you where you need to go."

Conclusion

Legacy and Impact

In 2025 Lamar kicked off the Grand National Tour, which he co-headlined with singer-songwriter SZA. The stadium tour spanned thirty-nine shows across North America and Europe. Lamar has remained quiet about any future music plans, but there is speculation that he is working on a new album or collaboration.

No matter what he does next, Lamar has undeniably and permanently impacted hip-hop and music culture. As one of the most influential rappers of his generation, he has redefined storytelling in rap through his intricate lyricism, social consciousness, and innovative sound. From *good kid, m.A.A.d city* to *To Pimp a Butterfly* to *DAMN.*, his albums tackle issues such as systemic racism, self-identity, faith, and personal struggles, and have resonated with listeners worldwide. His 2017 Pulitzer Prize for *DAMN.* cemented his status as a

Lamar won several Grammys for his single "Not Like Us" at the 2025 Grammy Awards.

music legend when he became the first rapper to receive the prestigious award.

Lamar's influence has reached beyond music into social movement and activism. Several of his songs, including "Alright," have become anthems for movements, such as Black Lives Matter, that aim to empower marginalized communities. He has also given back to his hometown of Compton through philanthropy by supporting education, youth programs, and local initiatives.

Lamar has inspired a new generation of musicians to embrace authenticity, vulnerability, and powerful storytelling. People often view him as a modern-day poet whose work challenges listeners to think about the world around them. He continues to make music that will add to his legacy. In taking his place as one of the greatest and most respected figures in hip-hop, Kendrick Lamar has become a global icon for people worldwide.

GLOSSARY

authenticity: being true to who you are and not pretending to be someone else

cadence: the rhythm or beat in how something is said or played

collaborate: to work together to create something

debut: an artist's first album or artistic work

discourse: talking or writing about a topic in a deep way

epiphany: a moment when you suddenly understand something important

exploitation: taking advantage of someone or something

funk: a type of music that's rhythmic and energetic, often with a lot of energy and groove

hype: excitement or attention given to something

iconic: something that is very famous or represents something important

innovative: coming up with new and creative ideas

mainstream: the principal current or direction of activity or influence. Mainstream media, such as music, is thought to be common or well-known in popular culture.

marginalized: when a group of people is treated as less important or pushed to the edges of society

mass incarceration: when a large number of people are put into prisons, often unfairly

MC: short for master of ceremonies and sometimes spelled emcee, a rapper with immense performance skill

mixtape: a collection of songs, usually made by someone to share with others

prestigious: being respected or admired by many people

redemption: the chance to make things better after making a mistake

repentance: feeling sorry for something wrong you've done and trying to change

stigma: a negative attitude or belief about something or someone

systemic oppression: when unfair treatment happens because of rules or systems in society

track: a single song or piece of music

SOURCE NOTES

7 "It's one of . . . hip-hop in general.": Lisa Robinson, "Cover Story: The Gospel according to Kendrick Lamar," *Vanity Fair*, June 28, 2018, www.vanityfair.com/style/2018/06/kendrick-lamar-cover-story.

11 "Admittedly, it done . . . get used to.": "Kendrick Lamar: 'I Can't Change the World until I Change Myself First,'" NPR, December 29, 2015, www.npr.org/2015/12/29/461129966/kendrick-lamar-i-cant-change-the-world-until-i-change-myself-first.

13 "You could put . . . I liked that.": Josh Eells, "The Trials of Kendrick Lamar," *Rolling Stone*, June 22, 2015, www.rollingstone.com/music/music-news/the-trials-of-kendrick-lamar-33057/3/.

16 "Everyone back then . . . somebody his age.": Marcus J. Moore, *The Butterfly Effect: How Kendrick Lamar Ignited the Soul of Black America* (Atria Books, 2020), 46.

22 "It was a . . . without a story?": "2009 Interview with Kendrick Lamar: From K. Dot to Kendrick," *West Coast Styles*, September 8, 2020, westcoaststyles.com/interviews/2020/09/994/.

26 "He had no . . . ourselves as individuals.": Erika Ramirez, "Kendrick Lamar Talks 'Section.80,' New Album and Upcoming Videos," *Billboard*, September 2, 2011, www.billboard.com/music/music-news/kendrick-lamar-talks-section80-new-album-and-upcoming-videos-467608/.

26–27 "I don't really . . . it out together.": Ramirez.

28 "When I go . . . good to me.": Ramirez.

33 "The story is . . . breathe with it.": Insanul Ahmed, "The Making of Kendrick Lamar's '*Good Kid, M.A.A.d City*,'" *Complex*, October 23, 2012, www.complex.com/music/a/insanul-ahmed/the-making-of-kendrick-lamars-good-kid-maad-city.

34 "This autobiographical intensity . . . up alongside him.": Jayson Greene, "Kendrick Lamar: *Good Kid, M.A.A.d City*," *Pitchfork*, October 23, 2012, pitchfork.com/reviews/albums/17253-good-kid-maad-city/.

40 "I mean, it's . . . only hire me.": "'Hypocrisy' in New Kendrick Lamar Lyrics Has Fans Debating," *The Seattle Globalist*, February 13, 2015, seattleglobalist.com/2015/02/12/kendrick-lamar-blacker-the-berry-song-controversy/33692.

43 "Music uplifts our . . . a rallying cry.": Jessica Mckinney, "The History of Kendrick Lamar's 'Alright' as a Protest Song," *Complex*, June 17, 2020, www.complex.com/music/a/j-mckinney/kendrick-lamar-alright-protest-song.

43 "*To Pimp a* . . . short of genius.": Micah Singleton, "*To Pimp a Butterfly*: Kendrick Lamar's New Album Is Perfect," *The Verge*, March 19, 2015, www.theverge.com/2015/3/19/8257319/kendrick-lamar-album-review-to-pimp-a-butterfly.

50 "I had heard . . . it was spectacular.": Andrew Barker, "How Kendrick Lamar Became the Defining Hip-Hop Artist of His Generation," *Variety*, November 21, 2017, variety.com/2017/music/features/kendrick-lamar-career-damn-to-pimp-a-butterfly-1202619725/.

55 "[The film's themes] . . . out and explore.": Jamie Atkins, "'Black Panther': How Kendrick Lamar Created a Musical Wakanda," UDiscover Music, March 8, 2023, www.udiscovermusic.com/stories/black-panther-soundtrack-feature/.

55 "It was something . . . the same music.": Atkins.

60 "As I produce . . . importantly, the Brotherhood.": Kendrick Lamar, "Nu Thoughts," oklama, August 20, 2021, https://oklama.com/nuthoughts.

60 "I don't even . . . and venture out.": "Punch on TDE's Transformation, SZA's Growth, and Kendrick Lamar's Swan Song," Mic, February 18, 2022, www.mic.com/culture/tde-punch-sza-kendrick-lamar.

62 "It's stuff that . . . up to 35.": Briana Younger, "Kendrick Lamar's Life Lessons," *W Magazine*, October 11, 2022, www.wmagazine.com/culture/kendrick-lamar-interview-2022.

63 "*Mr. Morale* & . . . name of truth.": Lucien Clough, "Kendrick Lamar Chooses Himself on 'Mr. Morale and the Big Steppers,'" *The Spectator*, 2025, https://stuyspec.com/article/kendrick-lamar-chooses-himself-on-mr-morale-and-the-big-steppers-2caf8fbf-645d-41ec-823f-989ada5912e6.

64 "I got love . . . heard of you.": "Drake and Kendrick Lamar's Beef — from Its Beginnings to the Super Bowl — Explained," WTHR, February 5, 2025, www.wthr.com/article/sports/nfl/superbowl/drake-kendrick-lamar-beef-explained/507-c2d38305-01b2-49ca-aeab-9996263c60b4.

67 "This is what . . . need to go.": "Kendrick Lamar Sweeps the 2025 GRAMMYs with Song of the Year Win," Grammy Awards, February 3, 2025, www.grammy.com/news/kendrick-lamar-not-like-us-wins-song-of-the-year-2025-grammys.

SELECTED BIBLIOGRAPHY

Associated Press. "Drake and Kendrick Lamar's Beef—from its Beginnings to the Super Bowl—Explained." WTHR. Last updated February 7, 2025. https://www.wthr.com/article/sports/nfl/superbowl/drake-kendrick-lamar-beef-explained/507-c2d38305-01b2-49ca-aeab-9996263c60b4.

Barker, Andrew. "How Kendrick Lamar Became the Defining Hip-Hop Artist of His Generation." *Variety*, November 21, 2017. https://variety.com/2017/music/features/kendrick-lamar-career-damn-to-pimp-a-butterfly-1202619725/.

Browne, David. "Kendrick Lamar's 'DAMN.': Inside the Making of the Number One LP." *Rolling Stone*, May 1, 2017. https://www.rollingstone.com/music/music-features/kendrick-lamars-damn-inside-the-making-of-the-number-one-lp-128446/.

Carmichael, Rodney, and Sidney Madden. " 'Black Panther: The Album' Is Kendrick Lamar's Parallel, Pan-African Universe." NPR, February 21, 2018. https://www.npr.org/sections/allsongs/2018/02/21/587331273/black-panther-the-album-is-kendrick-lamar-s-parallel-pan-african-universe.

Coscarelli, Joe. "Kendrick Lamar Wings Pulitzer Prize in 'Big Moment for Hip-Hop.' " *The New York Times*, April 16, 2018. https://www.nytimes.com/2018/04/16/arts/music/kendrick-lamar-pulitzer-prize-damn.html.

Jackson, Mitchell S. "Kendrick Lamar's New Chapter: Raw, Intimate and Unconstrained." *The New York Times*, December 27, 2022. https://www.nytimes.com/2022/12/27/magazine/kendrick-lamar-dave-free.html.

Limbong, Andrew. "Both Party and Protest, 'Alright' Is the Sound of Black Life's Duality." NPR, August 26, 2019. https://www.npr.org/2019/08/26/753511135/kendrick-lamar-alright-american-anthem-party-protest.

Reeves, Mosi. "Mixtape Primer: Reviewing Kendrick Lamar's Pre-Fame Output." *Rolling Stone*, July 14, 2017. https://www.rollingstone.com/music/music-album-reviews/mixtape-primer-reviewing-kendrick-lamars-pre-fame-output-126139/.

Shanfeld, Ethan. "Kendrick Lamar's 'Good Kid, M.A.A.D. City' Spends 10 Consecutive Years on *Billboard* Album Chart." *Variety*, October 20, 2022. https://variety.com/2022/music/news/kendrick-lamar-good-kid-10-years-maad-city-billboard-charts-1235410334/.

FURTHER INFORMATION

BOOKS

Bach, Greg. *Kendrick Lamar.* Mason Crest, 2025.
This biography gives readers a glimpse into the life and music career of rapper Kendrick Lamar.

Lewis, Miles Marshall. *Promise That You Will Sing About Me: The Power and Poetry of Kendrick Lamar.* St. Martin's Press, 2021.
This biography takes a deep dive into how Lamar came to be who he is today, his world, and how he creates his lyrics and music.

Markovics, Joyce L. *Kendrick Lamar.* Cherry Lake, 2023.
Readers can learn more about the life and career of Lamar in this biography.

Mooney, Carla. *Taylor Swift: Queen of Reinvention.* Twenty-First Century Books, 2025.
Readers can learn more about the life and career of Taylor Swift in this biography.

Schwartz, Heather E. *Kendrick Lamar: Platinum Rap Artist.* Lerner Publications, 2024.
Readers can follow Lamar's life story in this biography covering his childhood to his award-winning career.

Shepherd, Crown. *Hip-Hop Music: Songs That Changed the World.* Lerner Publications, 2025.
Readers can explore the hip-hop songs that have had an impact on the world, including some by Lamar.

WEBSITES

Billboard
https://www.Billboard.com/
The *Billboard* website has the latest news and information about the music industry, including the latest charts.

Grammy Awards
https://www.grammy.com/
The Grammy Awards is an annual awards show, and its website provides information about past and present nominees and winners.

HipHopDX
https://hiphopdx.com/
HipHopDX is an online magazine of hip-hop music criticism and news.

oklama
https://oklama.com/
Lamar's latest website has been used to release news about upcoming projects.

Rap-Up
https://www.rap-up.com/
Rap-Up is a national hip-hop and R&B magazine that features the latest news and information on music's biggest stars.

INDEX

Academy Awards, 53
  Best Original Song, 56
Aftermath Entertainment, 24, 31
albums
  Black Panther: The Album, 56, 58
  DAMN., 5–6, 49, 51–52, 55, 58, 68
  GNX, 65, 67
  good kid, m.A.A.d. city, 31
  Mr. Morale & the Big Steppers, 57, 61, 63
  Section.80, 25–27, 29–30
  To Pimp a Butterfly, 40–41, 43, 45, 53, 68
Alford, Whitney, 57, 60
Antonoff, Jack, 65
Baby Keem, 59

BET Awards, 43
Black Lives Matter movement, 41, 69
Black Panther, 53, 55–59

Cheadle, Don, 51
children, 57
Cleveland State University, 42
Club Paradise Tour, 31
Compton, California, 8–9, 11, 13–15, 25, 28–30, 33, 55, 57, 61, 69
Coogler, Ryan, 53

diss tracks, 64, 67
DJ Dahi, 48, 62
DMX, 36
Drake, 31, 64–65, 67
Dr. Dre, 13, 22, 24, 33, 39, 59
Duckworth, Kenny, 8, 11

50 Cent, 16, 32, 59
Free, Dave, 16, 18–19, 58
freestyle rap, 23

gang violence, 13–15, 33, 40–41
Grammy Awards
  Album of the Year, 5, 52, 56, 63
  Best Music Video, 52, 67
  Best New Artist, 35
  Best Rap Album, 35, 37, 45, 52, 63
  Best Rap Performance, 35, 45, 63, 67
  Best Rap Song, 45, 52, 63, 67
  Record of the Year, 52, 67
  Song of the Year, 56, 67

hiatus, 58, 61

Independent Grind Tour, 22, 25
Inge, Regis, 13
Interscope Records, 31–32, 50, 65

Kid Capri, 47–48

Macklemore, 37
Mandela, Nelson, 38
Martin, Terrace, 39
Martin, Trayvon, 40
mixtapes, 17, 19–23, 25, 48
  Kendrick Lamar EP, 22, 25, 57
  Overly Dedicated, 22, 25
Mustard, 65

oklama, 60
Oliver, Paula, 8–9, 11

pgLang, 58–59, 65
poetry, 13
profanity, 27
Pulitzer Prize, 5–6, 52, 68

Shakur, Tupac, 11–13, 20
songs
"All the Stars," 56
"Alright," 41–43, 45
"Bad Blood," 44
"Crown," 62
"Father Time," 62
"HiiiPoWeR," 29
"Keisha's Song (Her Pain)," 29
"King's Dead," 56
"Mother I Sober," 62
"Not Like Us," 65, 67
"Ronald Reagan Era (His Evils)," 29
"The Blacker the Berry," 40, 45
Sounwave, 48, 55, 61–62
South Africa, 38
spirituality, 48
Super Bowl, 59, 66
Swift, Taylor, 44, 64, 67

Tiffith, Anthony, 18–20
Top Dawg Entertainment (TDE), 18, 20–22, 24, 27, 31, 60–61, 65, 67

West, Kanye, 12, 20, 38, 67

ABOUT THE AUTHOR

Carla Mooney is a graduate of the University of Pennsylvania with a degree in economics. Today, she writes for young people and is the author of many books for young adults and children. Mooney enjoys listening to many genres of music, including Lamar's groundbreaking rap.

PHOTO ACKNOWLEDGMENTS

Image credits: Gregory Shamus/Getty Images, p. 4; Jeff Kravitz/Film Magic/Getty Images, p. 6; Kevin Mazur/Getty Images, p. 7; MattGush/iStock/Getty Images, p. 9; VALERIE MACON/AFP/Getty Images, p. 10; Al Pereira/Michael Ochs Archives/Getty Images, p. 12; Raymond Boyd/Michael Ochs Archives/Getty Images, p. 14; Jason LaVeris/FilmMagic/Getty Images, p. 17; Frazier Harrison/Getty Images, p. 18; Noel Vasquez/GC Images/Getty Images, p. 19; Earl Gibson/BET/Getty Images, p. 21; Paul R. Giunta/Getty Images, p. 23; Mike Coppola/Getty Images, p. 24; Roger Kisby/Getty Images, p. 26; Joey Foley/FilmMagic/Getty Images, p. 28; C Flanigan/FilmMagic/Getty Images, p. 32; Johnny Nunez/WireImage/Getty Images, p. 34; Christie Goodwin/Redferns/Getty Images, p. 35; Gregory Bojorquez/Archive Photos/Getty Images, p. 36; Michael Tran/FilmMagic/Getty Images, p. 37; Christopher Polk/Getty Images, p. 39; Mike Pont/Getty Images, p. 41; Angelo Merendino/Getty Images, p. 42; Kevin Mazur/WireImage/Getty Images, p. 44; Kevork Djansezian/Getty Images, p. 45; Theo Wargo/WireImage/Getty Images, p. 47; Christopher Polk/Getty Images, p. 49; Kevin Mazur/Getty Images, p. 50; Ollie Millington/Redferns/Getty Images, p. 51; Prince Williams/WireImage/Getty Images, p. 54; Allen J. Schaben/Los Angeles Times/Getty Images, p. 56; Lester Cohen/Getty Images, p. 57; Timothy Norris/Getty Images, p. 58; Ronald Martinez/Getty Images, p. 59; Kevin Winter/Getty Images, p. 63; Jamie Squire/Getty Images, p. 66; Monica Schipper/Getty Images, p. 69.

Cover: Gregory Shamus/Getty Images